MW00980916

paperblanks™
FABULOUS FOOTWEAR

High-Button Boots

This show stopping coral red button boot dates to the late 1890's. The exceedingly high heel, ornate gilt kid embellishment, and twenty-four open work gilt buttons were all clearly meant to attract attention.

Cette impressionnante botte à boutons de couleur rouge corail date de la fin des années 1890. Le talon extrêmement haut, les ornementations délicates en chevreau doré et les vingt-quatre boutons dorés ajourés étaient tous sûrement prévus pour attirer l'attention.

Dieser Furore machende Schnürstiefel in Korallenrot stammt aus den 90er-Jahren des 19. Jahrhunderts. Der ungewöhnlich hohe Absatz, die detailreichen Verzierungen aus Kalbsleber und die 24 vergoldeten, durchbrochen gearbeiteten Stiefelknöpfe dienten umissverständlich dazu, auf die Trägerin aufmerksam zu machen.

Deze oogverblindende koraalrode laars dateert van het laatste decenium van de 19de eeuw. De extreem hoge hak, de rijk vergulde versierselen en de vierentwintig opengewerkte gouden knoopjes zijn duidelijk bedoeld om de aandacht te trekken.

Estas espectaculares botas de botones de coral rojo datan de los años 1890. El tacón exageradamente alto de las botas de piel y sus elaborados adornos dorados con veinticuatro botones abiertos fueron claramente realizados para llamar la atención.

Calzatura rosso corallo dei tardi anni '90 dell'Ottocento dal taglio assai coprente. Il tacco straordinariamente alto, la pelle di capretto riccamente ornata e ventiquattro bottoni dorati che fermano un lembo traforato avevano il chiaro scopo di attirare l'attenzione.

ISBN 1-55156-276-6   160 PAGES   LINED

Photo used by permission of Bata Shoe Museum © 2002
© 2002 Hartley & Marks Publishers Inc. All rights reserved.
Paperblanks™ are published by Hartley & Marks Publishers Inc.
The text paper is an acid-free, archival quality sheet.
No part of this book may be reproduced without written
permission from the publisher. Made in China.
North America 1-800-277-5887
Europe +800-3333-8005

www.paperblanks.com